# Relapse and Repeat

Poetry by Elizabeth Valencia

Relapse and Repeat

Elizabeth Valencia

# You're worth it

# Relapse and Repeat

Elizabeth Valencia

Stay comparing me to them
  they are yours
        I'm not
  they are good
        I'm not
  no — I am not like them
          you raised me to be the opposite

*Relapse and Repeat*

I need it
I thought I could fight it
but I can't

Just one...
one cut

I just need to bleed
Please forgive me for this
I tried

*Elizabeth Valencia*

I hate seeing you hurt
I want to save you
But I can't
you put me in a position
Where it's me or you
People won't let me save you

I hate being selfish

No one has ever seen that side of you
  they have seen you naked
  but they haven't seen into your soul
if they did
   it wouldn't be so
        easy

                    for them to walk away

*Elizabeth Valencia*

What pain do you see
  it is different than what I feel

What? Do I look happy?
  I don't feel it
  you can't understand until you have felt it
  everyone feels pain different

mine is just harder to read

I wonder
what your thoughts are at night
and if they are similar to mine

I wonder
if you wonder if I'm ok
the way I wonder about you

I wonder
if you notice me

*Elizabeth Valencia*

They ask what I need
and I tell them
          *nothing*
  I need to feel nothing
  I need to stop my heart
    Can you help with that?
but of course I stop talking at
  *nothing*
                              it's an answer they are satisfied with

Our talks have been surface level
like the cuts on my wrist
but I could never get deep with you
like the ones on my legs
I know you think we have a connection
but I disagree
you know what I've been through
you don't know me

*Elizabeth Valencia*

Why does it feel wrong
to say *I love you*
I don't expect a response
or an embrace
even if we haven't seen each other
in months
to be honest I feel like you
don't care
though I would never say that
you have never been the type to show emotions
you might be my dad
but right now —
you feel like a stranger

If I stay
will you care
If I try
will you notice
all I need is a little bit of validation
for someone to say

*I see you*
*and I know it's hard*

cause I feel like I'm alone
in the suffering I feel
Maybe *alone* isn't the right word

I feel —
misunderstood

I know I'm not alone in that
but what if all the
misunderstood people
stood together?

then no one in the world
would be alone

*Elizabeth Valencia*

you know when your walls are so high
  you can't cry

but you feel it on the inside
        all the way in my fingertips
                when you cry on the inside

 that's how I felt
when I disappointed you

## *Relapse and Repeat*

*It's okay*
*I'm used to it*
she whispers

everyone leaves
they walk in and make a difference
but when they leave
I take 5 steps back from where I started
I'm used to the heartache
just promise me
when you leave
leave me with a part unbroken
so I can pick up the pieces

*Elizabeth Valencia*

I'm trying to challenge my thoughts
go against my worst nature
do the right thing

but what if the right thing
is removing myself from this
negative world

you call it
          selfish
I call it
          taking care of myself

I can write the words
*I love you*
a thousand times
and it won't make a difference
because your walls are up
and you will never let me in

*Elizabeth Valencia*

I'm scared
that if I let myself care
I will care too much
and fall apart
but there is no one here
to help put me back together
so I will stay broken

# *Relapse and Repeat*

Torn apart by the world
broken by their words
the pain of a teenager
the vocabulary of a child
yet it is enough to make someone
hate themselves
assuming their worth
they try to
kill themselves
the ones who succeed
didn't realize the impact
that they had
one death
led to another

all because you wanted
to put someone
down

I wanted to tell you
I swear I did
but for some reason
every time I opened my mouth
All I could say is
*I'm fine*

You know what I don't understand
you said you were scared of losing me
but I saw no fear
when you walked away from me
you must have gotten over it

*Elizabeth Valencia*

I thought I was past this
so why does it hurt
why do I not know how to make it stop
I thought I was past this
but when I close my eyes
I still see you

I keep falling
but I get up
even though I know I will fall again

why?

because no one is going to do it for me
so I had to learn to do it myself

*Elizabeth Valencia*

Yes you raised me
you taught me to fear company
you taught me to fear touch
I learned to
hate
everything I became
Yes —
you raised me
but I will always be
an orphan

It was the kind of pain
you fall to your knees from
but somehow
she got up
and when you asked
if she was okay
she smiled
but it didn't reach her eyes
and that's how you know
you broke her

*Elizabeth Valencia*

The castle you built
were from the stones they threw
but you built a shelter
the walls were their words
the paintings
your blood
and even though you felt
weak
You
stayed
alive

## *Relapse and Repeat*

I feel safe alone
I don't have to worry about
anyone else
I let my guard down
and I feel
pain
in the end even alone I'm not safe
I try to run
but the demons are faster
they whisper seductive words
in my ear
and in my heart
telling me I'm not alone
if I end my life

*jump*

they say and I put
the rope around my neck

*(snap)*

and I am left alone
in a darkness that I will never
get used to

*Elizabeth Valencia*

Don't try to relate to me
if you have never felt what I do
that shit hits deep
it's not fucking temporary
I feel it every day

you will never understand
how fucking hard it is
to want to be dead everyday

The sun rose
the leaves fell
and it was cold
that's how I remember
you

*Elizabeth Valencia*

Please
don't say that
I can't stomach the thought
she's not gone
it's a joke right
you're joking right

*No*

You hit me
 You starved me
  You hated me
So I tried to kill myself

But that's my fault —

right?

*Elizabeth Valencia*

Stop trying to save me
   You’re too late
I don't want to talk
I want to take these pills

and I won't feel better
      until I'm numb again

*Relapse and Repeat*

We live to die

So I apologize
for wanting to skip
to the end

*Elizabeth Valencia*

I look through my playlist
No song can explain what I feel

Does it mean
I've hit another level

I'm going to have to look deeper
Each word has a different meaning

A hidden message
Behind every smile

The words that I hear
*Will I ever be okay*

The smile I see
Is a reflection of my own

It reads *pain*

My mom died
they always look sad
but I never felt anything
Until now
Did you know you were gonna die?
Were you scared?
Why you?
He got 22 years
For something I lost my whole life

Elizabeth Valencia

Why do I come back?
        we fight
        we yell
        we throw things

but when you smile
it hits like the first time
and I could never leave

You said you're figuring yourself out
I'm happy for you
You need this
I hope you learn to love yourself
I never did
But maybe you could teach me

*Elizabeth Valencia*

What did I do?
Why can't I feel anything
I love it
I love being numb
It's the only time it's quiet

I'm just a pawn
A piece in your game
And I feel like shit
Because I actually cared

*Elizabeth Valencia*

Why do I write?

Because like you
I don't understand me
My hands work faster than my mind
        It's the only way I know what I feel

I didn't lose you
You lost me
You left

It's not me
It's you

*Elizabeth Valencia*

Seems like everything I do
  I do it wrong
my mouth still bleeds from
  the lies I told
I could get my shit together now
  but you wouldn't notice
you only see when I do wrong
I'm not going to waste my time
        trying to please you

## *Relapse and Repeat*

Today will be different
        I will smile
        I will laugh
        I will be ok
        I will be safe

I tell myself this every day
        I never believe it

*Elizabeth Valencia*

I'm sorry, I know how it feels to be taken
advantage of
I wish I could tell you it gets easier
  but I don't want to lie
      I understand
      you can't sleep
      you can't eat
      you can't love
      and that's ok
you have no idea how much I understand

*Relapse and Repeat*

I'm trying to
          hold my composure
                    stay calm
it's not that easy
why shouldn't I fuck shit up
it's been too long
          Why can't I stop caring?

Elizabeth Valencia

I'm scared

what if when I go home
 I’m not ready
   not better
and I fuck up
will you think I don’t care?

you don’t understand
how hard it is to stay stable
when you’re constantly reminded
          that you’re not

# *Relapse and Repeat*

I don't have a voice
I scream the words
        you don't hear
I write them down for you to read
        Then all of the sudden you're blind
What will it take
For me to be someone you will
Listen to
Me,
        your daughter

But that means nothing
        Does it?

*Elizabeth Valencia*

I hope I make it
I hope you make it
and I hope we do it all together

Crying isn’t weak
it's the realest emotion
the most vulnerable

it has the most beauty

it's ok

it wasn't you that made me cry
it was your words
and your actions
it wasn't

*you*

That didn't have to be it
        you could've stayed
        you should have continued to lie to me
at least your lies kept me sane

I did it again
I know I promised to stop
but I need it
It's self-punishment
I deserve to bleed
I just don't know how to stop

*Relapse and Repeat*

I need you to hate me
I need you to want me dead

it will be easier
        to stop caring
if you wanted me to

I accepted myself
I accepted the pain
I accepted the anger

now I hate the monster I became

We live by this rule
that we always have to be moving
it's no wonder your thoughts are loud
          you never stop to listen to what you need

*Elizabeth Valencia*

I am not a reflection of you
        I am him
every bad thing about him
        is me
and just like him

        I am alone because of it

## *Relapse and Repeat*

I am tired of writing my pain

Over
and over again

and still have no one understand

Elizabeth Valencia

You were my best friend
We played together in kindergarten

it's hard to believe
that the kid that was scared of swings
          was capable of rape

## *Relapse and Repeat*

I looked into his eyes and thought

*do it, I deserve it anyway*

cause being raped repeatedly just confirmed
what I already knew
this was my worth

Elizabeth Valencia

I look in the mirror disgusted with myself

and whisper
*I hate you*

then said
*I hate you*

then screamed
*I HATE YOU*

then watched as the glass shattered under my fist
as I held a piece to my throat

I whispered
*I'm sorry*

Falling in love with you
will always be the thing
that caused me
to hate
myself
because since you left
every part of me that you said was
beautiful
crumbled into nothing but
a mess
everything I took
pride in
became what I can't look at

*Elizabeth Valencia*

I am
what people look past

I'm invisible to the eyes that see
beauty

I am burned
I have no alive features

I am what people call
ugly

But —
          I am standing
when the beauty falls

do you really want to know
you always ask if I'm okay

here's the truth
I'm scared, I'm tired, and
I'm overwhelmed at the thought of staying alive

how are you?

*Elizabeth Valencia*

I hate what I am now
I hate that I don't care
I hate my anger
I hate myself
Every day I hit a new fucking low

When do I hit rock bottom?

I don't want to lose you
cause then I'd have to find me
        and I don't want to do that again

please stay
I like who I am with you

*Elizabeth Valencia*

Every day I tell myself
    that it's the last time

I've been doing that for 2 years now
    but every day I find a new way to fuck up

Safe or alone

What's the difference?

They both feel the same

*Elizabeth Valencia*

These words
are my cry for help
everything I write
is real for me
each letter
each word
is me asking for help
screaming for someone to notice that

I'm drowning
        and I don't want to fight for air

## *Relapse and Repeat*

When we fall apart
we never put ourselves together the same
all the pain changes us
the pain you left made me want to try
this time I'm someone I like
so thank you

for using me
for hitting me
for pretending you cared
for putting me back together

just to break me all over again
without you
I would still be disappointed
at my reflection

1 thousand apologies
        won't make it better

1 hundred I love yous
        won't change when you didn't

1 stay
        won't change my mind

You can tell by my words
and my actions
that I'm suicidal

you don't believe me
and that's okay

you will when I'm gone

*Elizabeth Valencia*

Then all of a sudden
the word *pain* or *broken*
didn't cover it
deep wasn't *deep* enough
*faded* didn't make me forget
the *telling* was *screaming*
all I wanted was for everything
to *stop*

so I ended it

I wish you were here
you would tell me
to smile
and that everything will be ok
you would hold me
and I would feel safe
right now I'm cold
and it's dark
and I miss you

my sun
my love
my safety

*Elizabeth Valencia*

I want you to know
        that I'm ok
I'm hurting and I'm sad
        but I'm ok
close your eyes beautiful
        and breathe
you deserve to sleep tonight

How can I make it better
I can't change the past
          but I want to
I'm breaking my back for you
          for your trust
          for your love
how can I fix this

Elizabeth Valencia

How much more can I take
	how much more till I break
	how much more till it's acceptable
	for me to kill myself
You have endured a lot
	you want me to stay?
	live with this pain every day?
I'm sorry
	let me tell you again
	I'm sorry
sorry I'm in pain
	sorry I can't stay
	sorry I'm not better
	sorry I'm not enough
	sorry I'm not strong
	sorry I gave up
Do you forgive me now?
	after all this time
do you get me now
	let me go
	let me die
	stop trying to save me

I'm already gone

I have a voice too
and I'm here
every imperfect
part of me
is asking you
to accept me

How do you walk away
from the person you love?
I want to do it for you
you call me selfish
but I don't ever want to hurt you

and if I stay
I will

I never used to be scared of the world
but one day it hit me
that people are ruthless
I used to stand against danger
but now —
        you will find me scared in the dark

*Elizabeth Valencia*

I feel like you're better without me
I feel like I lost myself in the battle
        I’m different now
        I’m scared
        I’m vulnerable
I forgot what it's like to feel
I'd give my life to be
numb again
        I miss being safe
        I miss being fearless
        I miss being alone

## *Relapse and Repeat*

Is no one near me?
I'm screaming for help
Does no one see me?
you keep walking when you see me cry
I'm invisible
alone
and misunderstood
to the point where people don't try to help
I'm a puzzle with a missing piece
unsolved and
worthless
left alone to collect dust
leaving me to wonder
would you notice if I was gone
no one wants something that's broken
no one loves something that's
gone

*Elizabeth Valencia*

In the middle of all the craziness

    the clouds parted
    and the rain stopped
    I took a minute to feel the sun
    and how warm it felt
then I looked into your eyes
 they are familiar and soft
I let myself feel loved
the security I feel now is different
    I'm not alone
the love in your voice reminds me
of why I'm trying
I step into your embrace
and I know
    I'm home
nothing felt better at this moment
then hearing you whisper

*I love you*

I watched you take your
last breath

when I took my first one

*Elizabeth Valencia*

I can't control it
it's like —
breathing
you do it once
then your mind doesn't let you stop

I knew it was a lie

but part of me was hoping
you wouldn't leave
that you would change your mind
and decide you actually loved me

*Elizabeth Valencia*

Please
make it stop
I can't do it
just make it all go away

I’m not as strong as I thought I was

Your once loving eyes
are cold
        please don’t do this
        I can't lose you too

Elizabeth Valencia

It's the type of pain you run from
it makes it hard to function
just don't take those pills
I promise the pain isn't real

Dear stranger
who made you take your walls down
when did you decide that you were worth it
who convinced you of that
I hope you know
that I've always seen it in you
the kind heart
the beautiful smile
and I was waiting for the day
that you saw it too
I want you to know
that I'm proud of you

Your words
were like music
your smile was seductive
everyone fell for you
and you had the whole world at your feet
but the beauty made you greedy
so you continued to fight for more
and when you found the one
you let her go
because she wasn't good enough for you
but she was
you just didn't see it
and now while you're alone
and humble
you wished you never let her go

I know I said I wouldn't
but I feel the need to drown for them
but in the end
who is going to drown for me

*Elizabeth Valencia*

Why do I still feel
so goddamn broken?

I did what I was supposed to
   I was vulnerable
   I was honest
   I was strong
yet at night
I pray I won't wake up

why is it so hard
to live?

I write words
people can relate to
they would think I've figured it out
but I'm still lost
and still suffocating
under my problems

*Elizabeth Valencia*

I found the company in myself
the silence left me comforted
        but I still remember
        how it felt
to be loved by someone
who showed me a light
that got stolen from
        depression

Help me
it’s hurting again
I don't know what happened
you didn’t catch me
like you said you would

help me
I’m broken again

The silence is more comforting
then your company
and that's hard
cause now I'm talking to my shadow

What kind of family is this
your love
        is a starved child
your affection
        are the marks you leave on your babygirl
you tell her all her mistakes
you point out her imperfections
then question why she is sad

        and tell her you gave her the world

*Elizabeth Valencia*

You said I was your other half
but there are a lot of pieces left behind

Which part did you mean?

Why me?
What is it that made you say

*You know what,*
*I'm going to hurt her*

why did you pick me
like I wasn't going through enough

It’s real
the good of it all
I didn’t know it at first
but this time it's different

I’m happier
because of you

Everyone is gone<br>
        they left<br>
I have never felt more alone<br>
you don't even look up<br>
when I say your name<br>
I see the pain in your eyes

I'm sorry<br>
I wish I could make it better<br>
but you don't need me

*Elizabeth Valencia*

Breathe beautiful
it's not easy, I know
when the world is loud and your mind is
screaming
it's all just noise
just close your eyes and count your heartbeat
you deserve to sleep tonight

## *Relapse and Repeat*

I am consumed by the constant feeling
that I will be left
when I was younger
I came to the conclusion that
if you don't let people in
they can't leave
but being alone
felt worse
so I let my guard down
for 2 people
I don't regret it
but I had to leave
so I made a promise and stuck with it
I'm tryna go back
but people against it
but I'm going to keep my head held high
show them that I've changed
I know I can do it
          but do they?

*Elizabeth Valencia*

It was like
waking up at 3 a.m. for a snack
or walking your dog
or petting your cat
it was like
sitting by a fire
on a cold night
it was a habit
and you were mine

## *Relapse and Repeat*

The fake smile fell
her strong posture broke
she fell to her knees
everyone stared at her shocked
        they saw her cry
        they saw her scars
        her bleeding heart
        her guard 100% down
she whispered

*I'm*
*not*
*okay*

this time they believed her
        it was the first time
they saw her broken
        it was the first time
she let them

If I tell myself
I'm ok
I'll start to believe it
but it doesn't change the fact
that every night
when the world is quiet
my head is screaming
that I need help

## *Relapse and Repeat*

I like my music loud
    it drowns out the thoughts

I like to be alone
    no one will question why I'm crying

I like drugs
    they make me happy

I like the thought of dying
    it means I won't feel pain

Elizabeth Valencia

Sometimes when I look at you
        I realize
I trust you because of your smile
I trust you because
I know you have been through a lot I have
and you're still struggling

Sometimes when I look at you
        I see pain
and I want to make it go away
but I know you can get through it

sometimes when I look at you
        I see strength
and I want to be as strong as you
and I know you're teaching me

sometimes when I look at you
        I remember why I'm fighting

I'm not bottling up
I just have watched everyone leave
I don't want to open up
just to lose you

*Elizabeth Valencia*

Look what you did to me

I use people
like you used me
that way
        I did it before they could

They don't understand
this message you put out
and that's ok
just remember who you are fighting for

I hate my scars<br>
all of them

but the ones you gave me

You said you love my eyes
you must not have seen

all the pain

*Elizabeth Valencia*

I get it now
I would have come back too
you feel like you deserve to be hit

don’t you

If you are there
I'm sorry
I'm going to do my best to give you
a good life
even if I couldn't do it for myself

Elizabeth Valencia

It's just one more skipped meal
until I'm perfect
one more cut
until I feel nothing
one more day
until it's over
one more smile
until I don't have to fake it anymore
one more pill
until I have enough
one more suicide attempt
until I'm dead

right?

Don't trust a smile<br>
a smile is easy to fake<br>
don't trust the words<br>
it's easy to lie<br>
don't trust the emotions<br>
they are easy to remember<br>
It's easy to convince people that you're ok

look into the eyes<br>
it's the only place you can't hide<br>
pain

Elizabeth Valencia

What if I admit that you're all I got
I guess you mean more than I thought
I regret wasting time when we fought
I know you regret getting caught
what if I don't stay
what if I take my life today
can you show me another way
I wish I could take back everything that happened
you can't take back what you said
would you care if you found me dead
that is not a threat
there is a lot I'm going through that you don't get
I guess I'm trying to pay my debt
I feel like part of you would be glad
you never thought I was sad
I know that I'm really bad
is there a part of you that regrets taking care of me
I said I was struggling in ways you couldn't see
I tried to be ok like you wanted me to be
I guess it's hard to believe
that even you gave up on me
so why should I try
you turned away when you saw me cry
you are a part of why I want to die
so I don't feel bad
this is for you mom and dad

## *Relapse and Repeat*

If I told you I'm scared
you might take advantage of it
you might give up when you're tired of my shit
you trust me but I don't trust you
you don't know me you just know what I've been through
half of it is from my parents so it's not true
the more I think the less I want you to know
I've been told I have to be vulnerable in order to grow
I'm in more pain than I'm willing to show
but this is my final option before I give up and die
I know I will fail so why should I try
I should just call my parents and say goodbye
or I can let my guard down and you see me cry
that will be hard for me I'm not going to lie
I want to be able to prove everyone wrong
I want to make it through this and show them I'm strong
what if I decide to let you in
I guess that's the only way I can win
I can show you my problems I hung on the wall with a pin
I know you know my stories all too well
they tried to tell you but it's mine to tell
what if I decide to take down my wall

*Elizabeth Valencia*

I can tell you my problems and watch them fall
I have to earn you my walls are tall
I know you have what it takes to help me through
it all
it's safe to say I know what to do
I'll take my walls down and open up to you

## *Relapse and Repeat*

I said I could do it
    I was wrong
    I don't want to feel this way anymore
    I don't want to cry
    I don't want to cut
    I don't want to breathe
    I'm tired of living this constant lie

that maybe one day
I will get better

*Elizabeth Valencia*

If the words
came as easy as the pain
  I'd be good at this
        but I'm only writing thoughts
I can't always put pain into words
  so I wear it instead

because I don't want to talk about it
and give it to someone else

I see beauty
in the hand you hold out
to the weak
I see strength
in the tears you shed
with people who need you
I see passion
in the way you forgive

so why is it
that if I hold up a mirror
you wouldn't see it too

who forgot to love you?

*Elizabeth Valencia*

Tell me one good reason
          convince me
why shouldn't I kill myself
it's been 5 years
I'm still not better
I'm tired of pretending I'm strong
this story doesn't have a happy ending

I'm meant to be a loss

I punish myself
    whether it's a blade to skin
    or sad music and a
    mental list of all the ways
I'm a fuck up

*Elizabeth Valencia*

I can't be what you want me to be
I'm scared of being a disappointment
buts it's unavoidable
        I'm nothing
        I'm a burden
        I'm dead on the inside
might as well be on the outside too

I smile
  when I'm in pain
I laugh
  when I want to cry
the pain is there
you just don't care enough
to see it

*Elizabeth Valencia*

*I love you*

I know
but you are 16 years
4 months
and 8 days too late
to press the eject button
on my life

## *Relapse and Repeat*

I hope at night
        when your hands reach across empty
sheets
and your mind
        brings back the memory of my smile
and you wish your eyes
        could follow the curves of my body

you are filled with regret and pain
you tried to cause me

It's not that you were meant for each other
or that she was “the one”

it’s the fact that you decided
that you didn’t want anyone else

you aren’t perfect for each other
but imperfections are irrelevant
when you love someone

You have said goodbye
so many times
that it doesn't hurt anymore

I want to be good enough
not only for you
but for me

www.ingramcontent.com/pod-product-compliance
Lightning Source LLC
LaVergne TN
LVHW010610160826
845677LV00013B/3346

* 9 7 9 8 8 4 4 0 8 5 4 7 5 *